D0563750

A Look at Teeth

By Allan Fowler

Consultants

Linda Cornwell, Learning Resource Consultant,
Indiana Department of Education

Jan Jenner, Ph.D.

Children's Press®
A Division of Grolier Publishing
New York   London   Hong Kong   Sydney
Danbury, Connecticut

Visit Children's Press® on the Internet at:
http://publishing.grolier.com

Designer: Herman Adler Design Group
Photo Researcher: Caroline Anderson

Library of Congress Cataloging-in-Publication Data

Fowler, Allan.
    A look at teeth / by Allan Fowler.
        p. cm. – (Rookie read-about science)
    Includes index.
    Summary: Discusses baby teeth and permanent teeth, the importance and uses
of teeth, and how they are used by different kinds of animals.
    ISBN 0-516-21217-6 (lib. bdg.)   0-516-26567-9 (pbk.)
    1. Teeth—Juvenile literature. [1. Teeth.] I. Titles. II. Series.
RK63.F   1999   98-46446
591.4—dc21   CIP
                                                         AC

Can you imagine eating without using your teeth? Most solid food must be chewed and to chew, you need teeth.

You also need teeth to talk clearly. Try saying the word "teeth" without touching your teeth with your tongue. It's impossible.

When you were a baby,
you didn't have any teeth.
That's why you had to eat
mushy baby foods.

Your first set of teeth
are called milk teeth or
baby teeth.

They started to come
in when you were about
6 months old.

You had all twenty milk
teeth by the time you were
about 2 1/2 years old.

You may already be losing
those milk teeth.

Your second set of teeth form under your milk teeth. When you are about 6 years old, they begin to push your milk teeth out.

Most people have twenty-eight second teeth by the time they are 13 years old. Your last four teeth—called wisdom teeth—will probably grow in by the time you are 21 years old.

The teeth in the front of your mouth have different shapes than those in the back of your mouth. That's because they have different jobs to do.

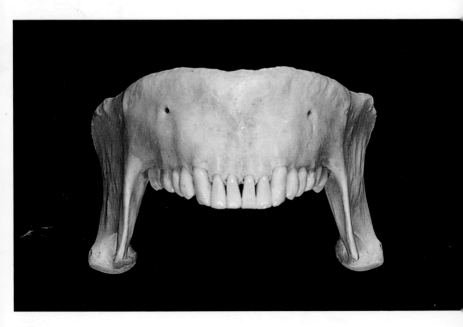

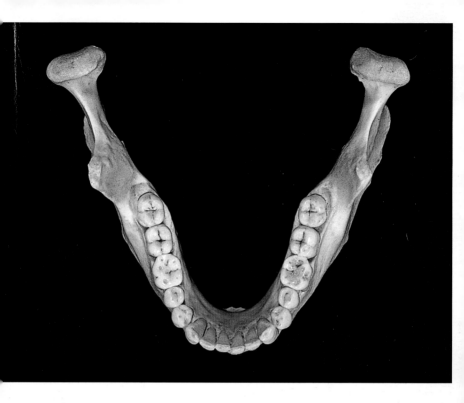

Your sharp front teeth are
used to bite into and cut
food. Your flatter back teeth
are used to grind food.

You are not the only animal
with teeth. Dogs, cats,
wolves, and lions have lots
of sharp, pointed teeth.

They use their teeth
to tear meat.

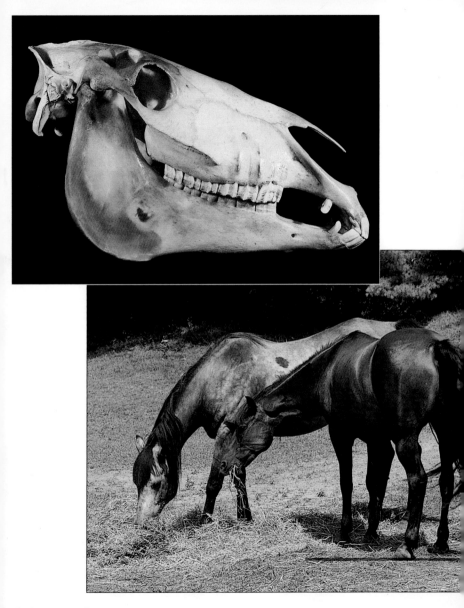

A horse's long front teeth are good for cutting hay.

Horses can grind hay with their flatter back teeth.

Elephants have teeth called
tusks. Tusks are so large
that they can't fit in the
animal's mouth.

An elephant's tusks can be up to 11 feet (3.3 meters) long.

Elephants aren't the only animals with tusks. Wild boars have small tusks that point upward.

Walruses have
very long tusks.

Some kinds of snakes have long, hollow teeth called fangs. When they bite an animal, poison flows out of the fangs and into the victim.

Animals use their teeth
for all sorts of things.
Hippopotamuses use
their teeth to fight.

Beavers use their teeth to cut down small trees.

They use the trees to build dams and dens.

A beaver's teeth wear down as it uses them, but that's not a problem.

The teeth keep on growing, so they are always sharp.

Sharks have as many as
twenty rows of teeth.
When old teeth break
off, new ones grow in.

If something happens to your second set of teeth, you can't replace them. That's why it's important to take care of them.

Don't forget to brush after meals, . . .

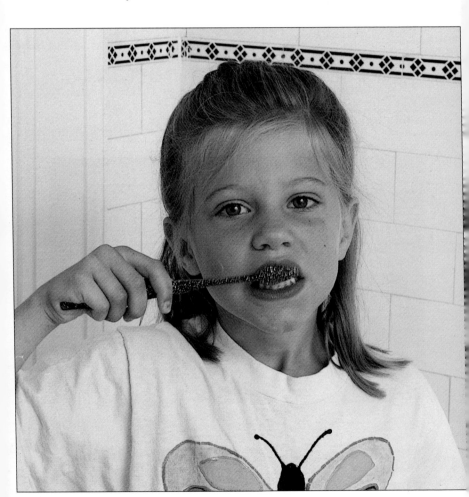

. . . floss every day, . . .

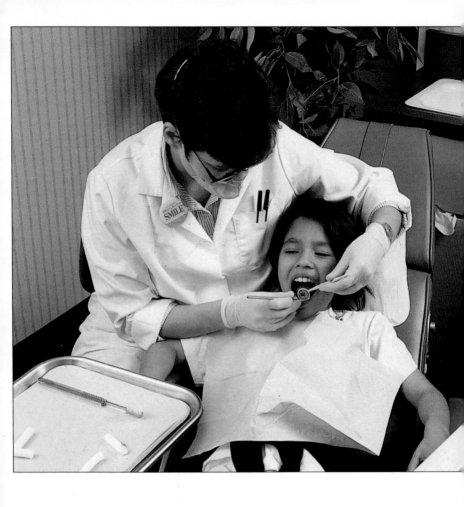

. . . and see your dentist
for a checkup twice a year.

Clean, healthy teeth give you something to smile about—and to smile with!

Words You Know

Milk teeth

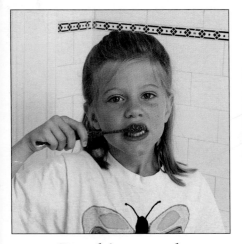

Brushing teeth

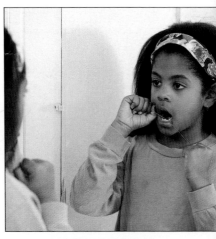

Flossing teeth

30

Beaver

Hippopotamuses

Shark

Walrus

Wild boar

Index

About the Author

Allan Fowler is a freelance writer with a background in advertising.
Born in New York, he lives in Chicago now and enjoys traveling.

Photo Credits